Brian D. Wheatley

To order additional copies of this book, contact:
Xlibris
844-714-8691
www.Xlibris.com
Orders@Xlibris.com

ISBN: Softcover   978-1-4691-5273-8
           EBook   978-1-6641-9534-9

Print information available on the last page

Rev. date: 10/20/2021

DEDICATION

I want to express my humble gratitude to my beautiful wife, Phyllis for her love and support and for continuing to believe in our dreams and in us; I love You! My deep love goes out to our two grown children, Gabrielle and Michael, who have been such an inspiration to me, as I have labored at times to turn my thoughts and feelings into words.

Thanks to God for giving me a message to write about and for the courage to share it with others.

To all those who have given Phyllis and me a chance to share our gifts and for all the encouragement you have provided, may rich blessings abound!

INTRODUCTION

In the times that we are living, we all need a place of Serenity where we can find a place of trust and hope.

May these offerings help you to find rest beneath the shadow of His wings, in the cleft of the Rock of Safety!

With peace and love!

Brian

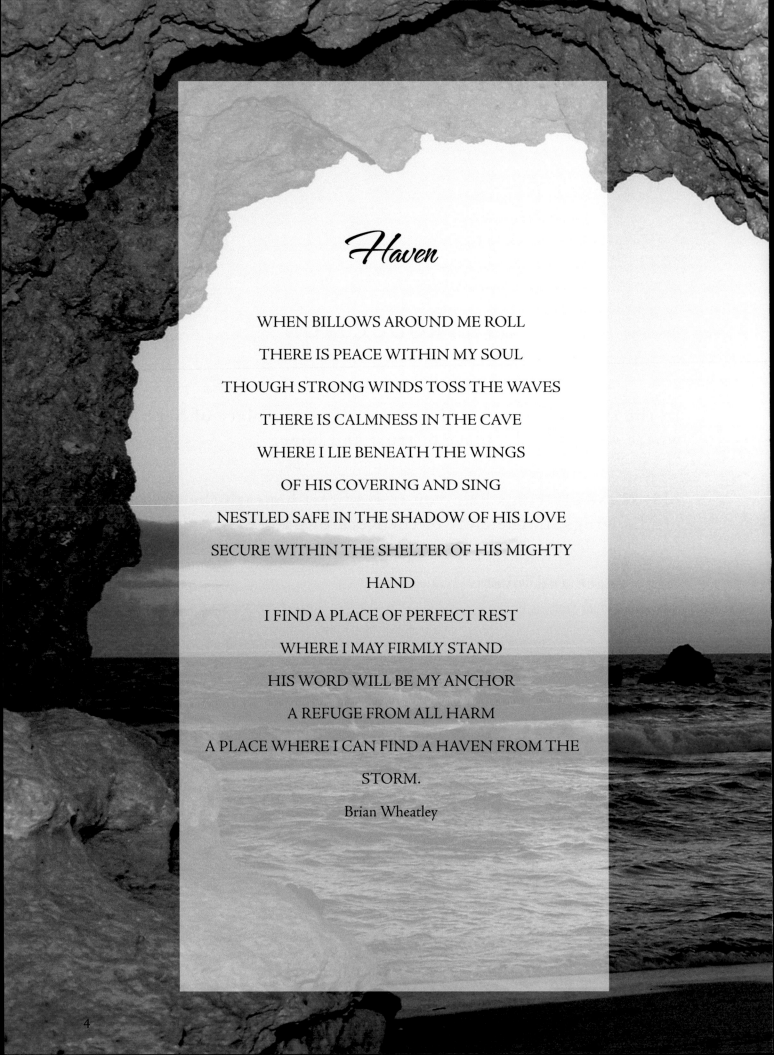

Haven

WHEN BILLOWS AROUND ME ROLL

THERE IS PEACE WITHIN MY SOUL

THOUGH STRONG WINDS TOSS THE WAVES

THERE IS CALMNESS IN THE CAVE

WHERE I LIE BENEATH THE WINGS

OF HIS COVERING AND SING

NESTLED SAFE IN THE SHADOW OF HIS LOVE

SECURE WITHIN THE SHELTER OF HIS MIGHTY

HAND

I FIND A PLACE OF PERFECT REST

WHERE I MAY FIRMLY STAND

HIS WORD WILL BE MY ANCHOR

A REFUGE FROM ALL HARM

A PLACE WHERE I CAN FIND A HAVEN FROM THE

STORM.

Brian Wheatley

Centurion's Song

IT WAS JUST A DAY LIKE ANY OTHER DAY

NOW THREE MORE MEN TO LEAD TO CALVARY

I HAD BEEN UP THAT HILL SO MANY TIMES

BUT THIS TIME WOULD BE DIFFERENT I COULD SEE.

THE GENTLE LOOK, THE KINDNESS SHONE FROM THIS

MAN'S FACE

THE TEARS THAT I SAW STREAMING FROM HIS EYES

STANDING THERE I COULD NOT KEEP FROM

WONDERING

WAS THIS MAN GUILTY OF A CRIME?

I WATCHED HIM AS HE PRAYED FOR THOSE WHO

MOCKED HIM THERE

AND I WAS TOUCHED SO DEEPLY THAT I CRIED

AS HE BOWED AND GAVE HIS SPIRIT UP TO GOD

THINGS BECAME SO CLEAR BY THE WAY HE DIED

HE LOOKED SO WONDERFUL

SO VERY DIFFERENT FROM ALL THE REST

I HAD SEEN SO MANY DIE BUT THIS JESUS WAS AS

GENTLE AS A LAMB

HE WAS SO WONDERFUL SO VERY DIFFERENT FROM

ALL THE REST

NOW I KNOW DOWN IN MY HEART GOD CARED

ENOUGH TO SEND HIS VERY BEST.

Brian Wheatley

He Is Alive Today

THEY TOOK HIS BODY DOWN

AND THEY LAID HIM IN THE GROUND

BUT THE GRAVE COULD NOT HOLD HIM

FOR SOON JESUS WOULD SHOW THEM

HE IS ALIVE TODAY

HE BOWED HIS HEAD AND DIED

THEY PIERCED HIM IN HIS SIDE

BUT EARLY ON THE THIRD DAY

ANGELS ROLLED THE STONE AWAY

HE IS ALIVE TODAY!

HE IS ALIVE TODAY!

THE TOMB NOW IS EMPTY

COME SEE THE PLACE WHERE JESUS LAY

FOR HE IS ALIVE TODAY!

Brian Wheatley

There He Was

SHE HAD FELT HIS TINY FINGERS CURLED AROUND HER

OWN

SHE HAD KISSED HIS BROW AND GENTLY HELD HIM

NEAR

AS SHE SAW THE SOLDIERS GAMBLE FOR HIS

ROBE

SHE COULD NOT KEEP HER MIND FROM GOING BACK

THROUGH ALL THOSE YEARS

TEARS FLOWED AS SHE WATCHED HIM TAKING HIS

FIRST STEPS

THE MEMORY OF HIS FIRST WORDS FILLED HER MIND

AND AS SHE STOOD BEFORE HIM

WATCHING AS HE DIED

SHE COULD NOT UNDERSTAND WHY THEY WERE ALL

SO VERY BLIND

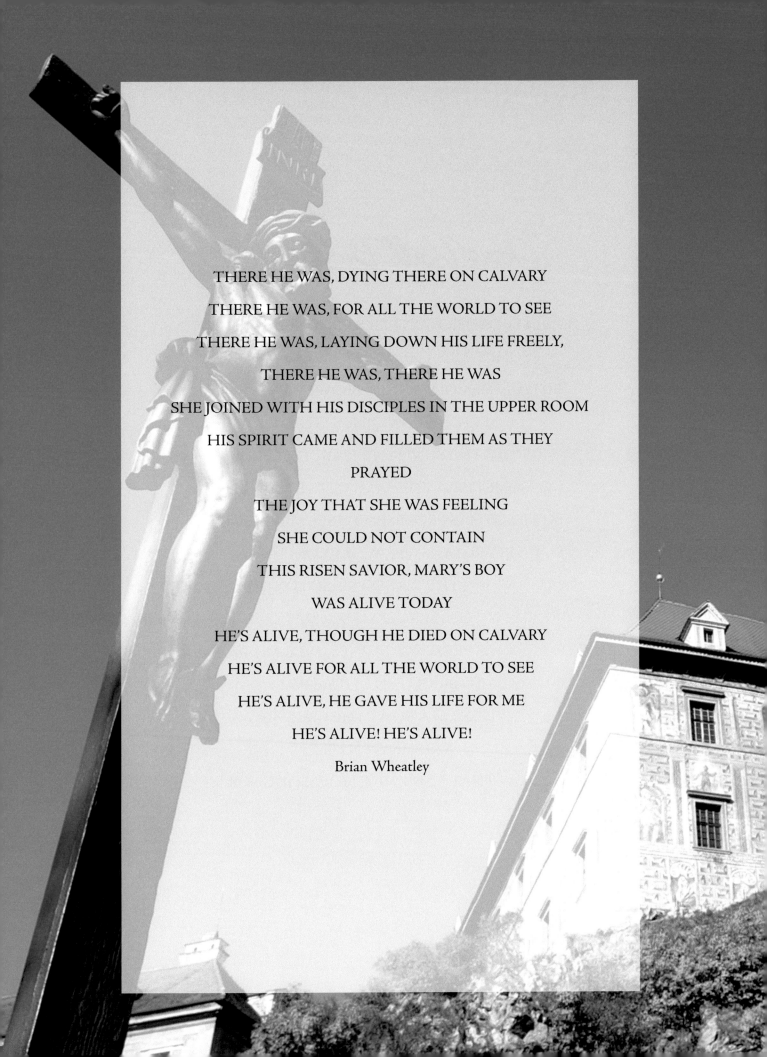

THERE HE WAS, DYING THERE ON CALVARY

THERE HE WAS, FOR ALL THE WORLD TO SEE

THERE HE WAS, LAYING DOWN HIS LIFE FREELY,

THERE HE WAS, THERE HE WAS

SHE JOINED WITH HIS DISCIPLES IN THE UPPER ROOM

HIS SPIRIT CAME AND FILLED THEM AS THEY

PRAYED

THE JOY THAT SHE WAS FEELING

SHE COULD NOT CONTAIN

THIS RISEN SAVIOR, MARY'S BOY

WAS ALIVE TODAY

HE'S ALIVE, THOUGH HE DIED ON CALVARY

HE'S ALIVE FOR ALL THE WORLD TO SEE

HE'S ALIVE, HE GAVE HIS LIFE FOR ME

HE'S ALIVE! HE'S ALIVE!

Brian Wheatley

Jesus Will Be Waiting

SOMETIMES THE WAY SEEMS SO LONELY AND COLD

SOMETIMES THE WAY SEEMS SO DREAR

BUT AS THE COLD WINDS BLOW OVER MY SOUL

I KNOW THAT JESUS IS NEAR

SOMETIMES THE SUNLIGHT IS HIDDEN FROM VIEW

SOMETIMES THE PATH GETS SO SMALL

BUT JESUS HAS PROMISED TO SEE ME THROUGH

HE WILL ANSWER WHENEVER I CALL

WHEN THE WAY SEEMS SO LONELY

THE SKY SEEMS SO GRAY

HIS PRESENCE SHINES OVER ME

TO BRIGHTEN UP THE WAY

WHEN I STAND AT THE CROSSING

AND HEAVEN I SEE,

I KNOW THAT JESUS WILL BE WAITING FOR ME

Brian Wheatley

Calvary's Lamb

I'M SO GLAD THAT JESUS FOUND ME

AND HE PARDONED ME BY GRACE

WHEN HE GAVE HIS LIFE FOR ME UPON THE TREE

ONE DAY I'LL GO TO SEE HIM, JUST TO LOOK UPON HIS
FACE,

THANKFUL FOR THE WAY HE BLED AND DIED FOR ME

OH WHAT MERCIFUL REDEMPTION

THAT CAUSED MY JESUS TO DIE

SO THAT WE COULD HAVE HIS PRESENCE EACH DAY

NOW MY GLADDENED HEART CRIES "GLORY!"

FOR THIS BLESSED JOY DIVINE

HE LAID DOWN HIS HOLY LIFE TO MAKE A WAY

OH GLORY HALLEUJAH! I'M RESTING IN HIS LOVE!

FOR ALL MY GUILT THE SACRIFICE WAS MADE

AND ONE DAY, I'LL GO TO LIVE IN MY FATHER'S
HOME ABOVE

FOR ALL MY SIN ON CALVARY'S LAMB WAS LAID

Brian Wheatley

Hold On To Yesterday

I DIDN'T GET A CHANCE TO SAY GOODBYE

NOW I'M HERE, TEARS IN MY EYES

REMEMBERING HOW IT WAS

YOU HAVE GROWN UP ALL SO FAST

MEMORIES, I KNOW NEVER LAST,

EXCEPT IN MY MIND

OH HOW I LOVE YOU

I'M ALWAYS THINKING OF YOU

EVEN THOUGH NOTHING STAYS THE SAME

AND AS YOU START YOUR DAY OUT THERE

I MUST OFFER UP A PRAYER

AS YOU MY BABY TURN TO WALK AWAY

I HOLD ON TO YESTERDAY

FUNNY HOW TIME GOES BY

AND SOON WE ALL MUST REALIZE

WE ALL HAVE A CERTAIN WORK TO DO

NOW IT SEEMS THAT MINE IS DONE

AND YOURS IS STARTING, FAR FROM WON

BUT I KNOW GOD'S GRACE WILL SEE YOU THROUGH

OH HOW I LOVE YOU!

I'M ALWAYS THINKING OF YOU

EVEN THOUGH NOTHING STAYS THE SAME

AND AS YOU LIVE YOUR LIFE OUT THERE

I STILL OFFER UP A PRAYER

AS YOU MY BABY KEEP THE FAITH

I HOLD ON TO YESTERDAY

Brian Wheatley

Healing Stream

I FEEL DIRTY, I FEEL OLD

I FEEL DARKNESS IN MY SOUL

UNTIL YOUR LIGHT FLOODS IN

AND WASHES IT AWAY

I'M TRYING TO FORGET

ALL THE HURT THAT CAME AND WENT

HOPING THAT THIS DAY WILL BE

A BETTER DAY

IN THIS LIFE I'VE BEEN ABUSED

OVERSPENT AND SO CONFUSED

WITH NO REST FROM ALL THE HASSLES

AND THE PAIN

BUT SOMEHOW I KNOW YOU'RE THERE

WHEN I CALL YOUR NAME IN PRAYER

WAITING PATIENTLY TO FEEL YOUR

TOUCH AGAIN

AS I RAISE MY VOICE UP TO THE SAINTS

AND ANGELS

BEGGING THEM TO COME AND EASE MY

TROUBLED MIND

THERE'S A PEACE THAT FALLS AND

SETTLES LIKE A MANTLE

FOR YOUR HEALING STREAM LEAVES

ALL MY PAST BEHIND

Brian Wheatley

I'll Be Your Daddy

IT'S BEEN A NUMBER OF YEARS

SINCE THEY PUT MY DAD DOWN

LAID HIM TO REST IN A HOLE IN THE

GROUND

AND MY HEART WAS SO NUMB BY THE PAIN

OF EVERYTHING

I CRIED OUT, LORD TELL ME WHAT WILL

I DO

NOW THAT HE'S GONE I MIGHT AS WELL BE

TOO

HOW AM I GOING TO MAKE IT UNTIL I GET

TO WHERE HE IS GOING?

HE SAID, I'LL BE YOUR DADDY, WHEN

YOU'RE ALL ALONE

WHEN YOU THINK YOU CAN'T MAKE IT

AND ALL HOPE IS GONE

IF YOU'RE OUT ON YOUR OWN

FACING THE STORM

JUST RUN INTO MY LOVING ARMS

I'LL BE YOUR DADDY,

I'LL KEEP YOU SAFE FROM HARM

NOW I AM A FATHER

WITH KIDS OF MY OWN

THERE'LL BE A TIME WHEN I MUST

MOVE ON

TO A PLACE THAT MY FATHER HAS

FURNISHED TO ME UP IN HEAVEN

WHEN MY TIME COMES

AND I HAVE TO GO

I WANT MY CHILDREN TO COME TO

KNOW

A DADDY WHO PROMISED TO BE BY

THEIR SIDE FOREVER

HE'LL SAY, I'LL BE YOUR DADDY

WHEN YOU'RE ALL ALONE

WHEN YOU THINK YOU CAN'T MAKE IT

AND ALL HOPE IS GONE

WHEN YOU'RE OUT ALL ALONE

FACING THE STORM

JUST RUN INTO MY LOVING ARMS

I'LL BE YOUR DADDY

ILL KEEP YOU SAFE FROM HARM

Brian Wheatley

Printed in the United States
by Baker & Taylor Publisher Services